The Making of Everyday Things

Pencils

Derek Miller

New York

Published in 2020 by Cavendish Square Publishing, LLC
243 5th Avenue, Suite 136, New York, NY 10016

Copyright © 2020 by Cavendish Square Publishing, LLC

First Edition

No part of this publication may be reproduced, stored in a retrieval system, or transmitted in any form or by any means—electronic, mechanical, photocopying, recording, or otherwise—without the prior permission of the copyright owner. Request for permission should be addressed to Permissions, Cavendish Square Publishing, 243 5th Avenue, Suite 136, New York, NY 10016. Tel (877) 980-4450; fax (877) 980-4454.

Website: cavendishsq.com

This publication represents the opinions and views of the author based on his or her personal experience, knowledge, and research. The information in this book serves as a general guide only. The author and publisher have used their best efforts in preparing this book and disclaim liability rising directly or indirectly from the use and application of this book.

All websites were available and accurate when this book was sent to press.

Library of Congress Cataloging-in-Publication Data

Names: Miller, Derek L., author.
Title: Pencils / Derek Miller.
Description: First edition. | New York : Cavendish Square, 2020. |
Series: Making of everyday things | Includes bibliographical references and index. | Audience: Grades K-3.
Identifiers: LCCN 2018047199 (print) | LCCN 2018053363 (ebook) | ISBN 9781502647016 (ebook) |
ISBN 9781502647009 (library bound) | ISBN 9781502646989 (pbk.) | ISBN 9781502646996 (6 pack)
Subjects: LCSH: Pencils--Juvenile literature.
Classification: LCC TS1268 (ebook) | LCC TS1268 .M55 2020 (print) | DDC 681/.6--dc23
LC record available at https://lccn.loc.gov/2018047199

Editorial Director: David McNamara
Copy Editor: Nathan Heidelberger
Associate Art Director: Alan Sliwinski
Designer: Ginny Kemmerer
Production Coordinator: Karol Szymczuk
Photo Research: J8 Media

The photographs in this book are used by permission and through the courtesy of: Cover Pam Walker/Shutterstock.com; p. 5 Fat Camera/iStockphoto.com; p. 7 Gregor Schuster/Photographer's Choice/Getty Images; p. 9 Gary Ombler/Dorling Kindersley/Getty Images; p. 11 LukeSharrett/Bloomberg via Getty Images; p. 13 Emile Wamsteker/Bloomberg/Getty Images; p. 15 VPC Photo/Alamy Stock Photo; p. 17 Philippe DesMazes/AFP/Getty Images; p. 19 Todd Kuhns/Shutterstock.com; p. 21 Emile Wamsteker/Bloomberg/Getty Images.

Printed in the United States of America

Contents

Pencils **4**

New Words **22**

Index **23**

About the Author **24**

People use pencils all the time.

We use them to write and draw.

Pencils look simple.

But they are hard to make.

Pencils have many parts.

Wood is on the outside.

Wood makes the pencil thicker.

This makes it easier to hold.

7

Pencils begin as **slats**.

Slats are flat pieces of wood.

Many pencils come from one slat.

9

A machine cuts **grooves** in each slat.

The grooves are for the **graphite**.

Graphite is gray.

Graphite is laid in each groove.

Graphite marks the paper.

It is called lead.

But it is made from graphite.

It comes from the ground.

13

Another slat is put on top.

The graphite is in the middle.

The two slats are glued together.

This keeps the graphite in place.

Now the slats are cut.

Many pencils are cut from one slat.

The pencils are almost ready.

The **ferrule** is stuck on the pencil.

The ferrule is the metal part.

The ferrule holds the eraser.

The eraser lets you change what you write.

19

Now the pencil is ready!

The wood makes it easy to hold.

The graphite leaves a mark.

People use pencils to write and draw!

New Words

ferrule (FEHR-uhl) The metal part on the end of the pencil.

graphite (GRA-fite) The gray part of the pencil that leaves a mark.

grooves (GREWVS) Long, narrow cuts.

slats (SLATS) Thin sheets of wood.

Index

eraser, 18

ferrule, 18

glued, 14

graphite, 10, 12, 14, 20

grooves, 10

lead, 12

machine, 10

slats, 8, 10, 14, 16

wood, 6, 8, 20

write, 4, 18, 20

About the Author

Derek Miller is a teacher and writer. He likes to learn interesting facts about things we see every day.

About

Bookworms help independent readers gain reading confidence through high-frequency words, simple sentences, and strong picture/text support. Each book explores a concept that helps children relate what they read to the world they live in.